Annette Wolter

Cover photograph by Paul Williams
Published on behalf of
The Boots Company plc Nottingham
by Hamlyn Publishing,
a division of The Hamlyn Publishing Group Ltd,
Bridge House, London Road, Twickenham, Middlesex, England

ISBN 0 600 32556 3

First published under the title
Die raffinierte Schnellküche

Set in 10 on 11pt Monophoto Sabon 669
by Tameside Filmsetting Ltd,
Ashton-under-Lyne, Lancashire

Printed in Italy

Contents

Useful facts and figures	6
Introduction	7
Fish and shellfish	8
Meat and poultry	13
Rice, pasta and potatoes	25
Salads	34
Snacks	40
Desserts	56
Index	63

Useful facts and figures

Notes on metrication

In this book quantities are given in metric and Imperial measures. Exact conversion from Imperial to metric measures does not usually give very convenient working quantities and so the metric measures have been rounded off into units of 25 grams. The table below shows the recommended equivalents.

Ounces	Approx g to nearest whole figure	Recommended conversion to nearest unit of 25
1	28	25
2	57	50
3	85	75
4	113	100
5	142	150
8	227	225
9	255	250
12	340	350
13	368	375
16 (1 lb)	454	450
18	510	500
20 (1¼ lb)	567	575

Note: When converting quantities over 20 oz first add the appropriate figures in the centre column, then adjust to the nearest unit of 25. As a general guide, 1 kg (1000 g) equals 2.2 lb or about 2 lb 3 oz. This method of conversion gives good results in nearly all cases, although in certain pastry and cake recipes a more accurate conversion is necessary to produce a balanced recipe.

Liquid measures The millilitre has been used in this book and the following table gives a few examples.

Imperial	Approx ml to nearest whole figure	Recommended ml
¼ pint	142	150 ml
½ pint	283	300 ml
¾ pint	425	450 ml
1 pint	567	600 ml
1½ pints	851	900 ml
1¾ pints	992	1000 ml (1 litre)

Spoon measures All spoon measures given in this book are level unless otherwise stated.

Can sizes At present, cans are marked with the exact (usually to the nearest whole number) metric equivalent of the Imperial weight of the contents, so we have followed this practice when giving can sizes.

Oven temperatures

The table below gives recommended equivalents.

	°C	°F	Gas Mark
Very cool	110	225	¼
	120	250	½
Cool	140	275	1
	150	300	2
Moderate	160	325	3
	180	350	4
Moderately hot	190	375	5
	200	400	6
Hot	220	425	7
	230	450	8
Very hot	240	475	9

Note: When making any of the recipes in this book, only follow one set of measures as they are not interchangeable.

Basic storecupboard

The following ingredients are ideal to keep in the storecupboard for quick dishes.

bread mixes
canned fruit, corned beef
dessert topping
flour – plain and self-raising
luncheon meat
pasta, pimientos, pineapple rings/crushed
rice
sardines, soup/condensed, canned and packeted, stuffing mix, sweet and sour sauce, sweet corn kernels
tomato purée
tuna/salmon

Introduction

Everyone has at some time been faced with having to prepare a meal in minutes, whether it is for a hungry family whose appetites won't wait, or for that unexpected guest who didn't really plan to stay for supper. You will be surprised at what can be done, given a little imagination, a few basic ingredients and the help and advice of a competent, experienced and inventive cook.

Annette Wolter has put together a clever collection of recipes especially for the cook in a hurry, and though they make full use of storecupboard items, they do not compromise on flavour. In fact, as Annette Wolter hails from Germany, many of the recipes have a continental touch.

The dishes themselves range from the unashamedly simple – a Sausage goulash that takes less than 10 minutes, to the deliciously sophisticated – a Festive scampi that would do justice to a gourmet's table. There's something to suit every occasion it be a quick, midday snack or a full evening meal. There's no need to feel that you must have a great deal of complicated cooking equipment at your disposal. A stove or ring, a pan or two, a can opener, blender and a small refrigerator, and you are ready to start. You can choose to make a main course and follow it with fresh fruit, cheese or ice cream, or plan on whipping up a speedy pudding – a Raspberry curd cheese or Mocha mousse – while family and friends relax between courses.

The recipes in each chapter, starting with Soups right through to Desserts, are schemed into three time zones: first, dishes that can be prepared in 5–10 minutes, then those that take 10–15 minutes, and lastly, the ones that take up to 25 minutes. The preparation times are stated at the head of each recipe to make it easy to plan and time a complete menu. These times have been carefully checked; however, no two cooks work at the same speed, and you will soon find how well the timing fits into your personal 'league table'. Chilling needs to be taken into account where it occurs, as precise times for this have not been included. So much depends on individual taste and whether you have a refrigerator or a freezer. When planning a menu, it could mean making a dessert first and leaving it to chill while you organise the rest of the meal.

Quick Dishes has all the answers for those whose idea of bliss is *not* spending hours and hours in the kitchen. Get to know it well, sample some of its imaginative and appetising dishes and you will never again feel that rising tide of panic as the doorbell rings and the hands on the clock show all too clearly that there isn't time to make the meal you had planned to serve.

Note: Each recipe in this book will serve four people

Fish and shellfish

Shrimp vols-au-vent

(Illustrated below)

Preparation time: 10-15 minutes

50 g/2 oz Edam cheese
4 individual vol-au-vent cases
1 (198-g/7-oz) can shrimps
200 g/7 oz canned mussels
100 g/4 oz canned carrots, diced
juice of ½ lemon
a little caviare or lumpfish roe to garnish (optional)

Set the oven at hot (230 C, 450 F, Gas Mark 8) or heat the grill to maximum. Slice half the cheese into four and put one piece of cheese in the bottom of each pastry case. Place in the oven just to heat through. Drain and rinse the shrimps under cold running water, reserving 8 to garnish. Drain the mussels and carrots. Cut the rest of the cheese into strips. Mix together the shrimps, mussels and carrots and fill the warm pastry cases with this mixture. Top with the cheese strips and place in the oven or under grill for 2–3 minutes. Garnish each with two of the reserved shrimps and sprinkle with caviare or lumpfish roe, if liked, before serving.

Festive scampi

(Illustrated opposite)

Preparation time: 10-15 minutes

15 g/½ oz butter
4 eggs
pinch each salt and pepper
4 large slices white bread
4 slices smoked salmon
4 scampi, cooked and peeled
1 tablespoon caviare or lumpfish roe (optional)

Melt the butter in a pan over gentle heat. Meanwhile, whisk the eggs in a bowl, season, then lightly scramble in the hot butter. When just set, divide the egg mixture between the bread slices. Roll up each slice of smoked salmon and place one on each slice of bread. Add one scampi to each and garnish, if liked, with a little caviare or lumpfish roe.

Below: Shrimp vols-au-vent; *Opposite:* Festive scampi.

Cod with creamed horseradish sauce

(Illustrated opposite)

Preparation time: 15-25 minutes

575 g/ 1¼ lb fresh cod fillets
½ teaspoon salt
2 teaspoons lemon juice
600 ml/ 1 pint water
100 ml/ 4 fl oz cider
2 slices lemon
bunch mixed fresh herbs
1 apple
75 g/ 3 oz grated horseradish or horseradish cream
pinch each salt and castor sugar
150 ml/ ¼ pint double cream
lemon wedges and parsley to garnish

Rinse fish under cold water and dry on absorbent kitchen paper. Rub with the salt and sprinkle with lemon juice. In a saucepan, bring the water and cider to the boil with the lemon slices and herbs. Add the fish and simmer over low heat for 15 minutes. Remove the fish and keep warm. Peel, core and grate the apple and mix with horseradish, salt and sugar. Whip the cream until stiff and fold in the apple and horseradish mixture. Garnish the fish with lemon wedges and parsley and serve with the accompanying sauce.

Baked fish fillets

Preparation time: 15-25 minutes

675 g/ 1½ lb fresh white fish fillets
1 tablespoon lemon juice
1 teaspoon salt
4 tablespoons water
300 g/ 11 oz canned button mushrooms
2 tablespoons chopped parsley
25 g/ 1 oz cheese, grated
15 g/ ½ oz butter

Set the oven at moderately hot (190 C, 375 F, Gas Mark 5). Place the fish on a plate, sprinkle with lemon juice and season with salt. Transfer to a shallow pan and steam or gently poach the fish, covered, in the measured water for about 10 minutes. Drain the mushrooms thoroughly. Arrange the cooked fish in an ovenproof dish, layer with mushrooms, and top with the parsley and cheese. Dot with the butter and bake in the oven for 8–10 minutes, or until the cheese has melted. Serve with rice or plain boiled potatoes and a crisp green salad.

Variation

The fish and mushrooms can be first heated through in the oven. Then add the butter and cheese, place under a medium-hot grill to brown.

Fish in white wine sauce

Preparation time: 15-25 minutes

150 ml/ ¼ pint water
½ teaspoon salt
1 tablespoon lemon juice
575 g/ 1¼ lb frozen white fish fillets
150 ml/ ¼ pint white wine
bunch fresh dill or parsley
2 egg yolks
100 ml/ 4 fl oz single cream
generous pinch of sugar

In a saucepan, bring the water to the boil with the salt and lemon juice. Lower the fish carefully into the water, cover and simmer for 12 minutes over gentle heat. Remove the fish, drain well and keep warm. Add the wine to the fish liquid and allow to come to a simmer. Wash, dry and chop the dill or parsley. Whisk the egg yolks with the cream and sugar. Beat 1 tablespoon of the fish liquid into the egg yolk mixture, then stir in the remaining fish liquid. Return to the saucepan and continue stirring until the sauce thickens but do not allow it to boil. Remove the saucepan from the heat, pour the sauce over the fish and sprinkle with dill or parsley before serving. Serve with Rice with mushrooms (see page 25) and a crisp green salad.

Cod with creamed horseradish sauce (recipe above).

Tuna vols-au-vent

Preparation time: 15-25 minutes

4 individual vol-au-vent cases
½ onion
1 (184-g/6½-oz) can pimientos
1 (198-g/7-oz) can tuna
4 eggs, hard-boiled
pinch each salt, pepper, paprika pepper and garlic salt
1 (198-g/7-oz) can shrimps
4 sprigs of parsley
lettuce leaves

Set the oven at moderately hot (190 C, 375 F, Gas Mark 5). Place the vol-au-vent cases on a baking sheet and heat gently in the oven. Meanwhile, peel and dice the onion, drain the pimientos and cut them into strips, reserving 4 to garnish. Drain the tuna well and flake with a fork in a bowl. Shell the eggs and chop them. Mix together the diced onion, pimiento strips, flaked tuna and chopped egg and season with salt, pepper, paprika and garlic salt.

Mix well and use to fill the vol-au-vent cases. Replace these in the oven to heat through. Meanwhile, drain and rinse the shrimps under cold running water. Pat dry on absorbent kitchen paper. Wash the parsley.

Garnish the warm pastry cases with the shrimps, the reserved pimiento strips and a sprig of parsley.

Lobster mayonnaise rolls

Preparation time: 15-25 minutes

1 pickled cucumber
bunch of parsley or dill
2 tomatoes
2 round crusty bread rolls
25 g/1 oz butter
2 tablespoons mayonnaise
2 tablespoons tomato ketchup
50 g/2 oz curd cheese
1 (225-g/8-oz) can lobster or crabmeat
½ lemon, sliced to garnish

Set the oven at hot (230 C, 450 F, Gas Mark 8) or heat the grill to maximum. Dice cucumber, wash and chop the parsley or dill. Wash and slice the tomatoes. Cut the bread rolls in half, hollow out and discard the soft middle and thinly spread the insides with butter. Place under the grill, cut side up, and lightly toast. Mix together the mayonnaise, ketchup, curd cheese and diced cucumber. Drain the lobster or crabmeat, rinse under cold running water, drain and flake with a fork. Blend into the mayonnaise mixture. Fill each warm, hollowed bread roll with lobster or crabmeat mayonnaise, garnish with parsley or dill and serve with a slice of lemon. Serve with Yogurt pea salad (see page 38).

Meat and poultry

Although grilling and frying meat are simple and quick methods of cooking, the time spent also depends on the quality of meat – good quality meat will cook evenly and faster than meat of a poorer standard. Remember, garnishes such as sprigs of parsley, dill or tomato slices are important as they turn a simple cooked dish into something special.

Sausage goulash

(Illustrated below)

Preparation time: 5-10 minutes

450 g/1 lb Frankfurter sausages
1 onion
1 (493-g/15.5-g) jar mixed pickles
2 tablespoons oil
1 (300-g/10-oz) can tomato soup
2 tablespoons tomato purée
salt and pepper
1 teaspoon dried marjoram

Slice the Frankfurters; peel and dice the onion. Drain the mixed pickles, then rinse briefly under cold running water and drain. Heat the oil in a saucepan or flameproof casserole and lightly fry the onion and mixed pickle. Add all the remaining ingredients and the Frankfurters to the onion mixture and stir well. Cover the pan and allow the goulash to simmer over a low heat for a further 5 minutes. Serve with plain boiled rice.

Sausage goulash.

Hunter's steak

(Illustrated opposite)

Preparation time: 10-15 minutes

2 tablespoons oil
4 (180-g/6½-oz) fillet steaks
½ teaspoon each salt and pepper
4 canned artichoke bottoms
4 eggs
1 (213-g/7½-oz) can button mushrooms, drained and chopped
2 tablespoons chopped parsley

Heat the oil in a frying pan and fry the steaks for 5 minutes on each side. Season with half the salt and pepper, remove from the pan and keep warm. Drain the artichoke bottoms. Whisk the eggs with the remaining seasoning. Heat the mushrooms in the frying pan with the fat left over from the steaks, pour in the egg mixture, and stir until set. Place artichoke bottoms around the edge of the frying pan to heat through. To serve, set one artichoke bottom on each steak and top with some of the egg and mushroom mixture. Sprinkle over the parsley before serving with a green salad and French bread.

Steak au poivre

Preparation time: 10-15 minutes

4 tablespoons white peppercorns
4 (200-g/7-oz) fillet steaks
2 tablespoons oil
½ teaspoon each salt and celery salt
15 g/½ oz butter
75 ml/3 fl oz brandy

Coarsely crush the peppercorns, using the flat of the blade of a sharp knife or a pestle and mortar. Gently press the steaks into the peppercorns so they coat the meat well on both sides. Heat the oil in a frying pan and briskly fry the steaks on both sides. When cooked enough to suit, season well. Pour out the oil from the pan and add the butter. Pour the brandy into a ladle, warm it slightly and carefully set it alight, pouring the flaming brandy over the steaks. After one minute, turn the steaks over to extinguish any remaining flame. Serve with French bread or potato chips and Green salad with mayonnaise sauce (see page 36). Follow with Vanilla ice cream with hot chocolate sauce (see page 58).

Classic steak

Preparation time: 10-15 minutes

4 (200-g/7-oz) steaks (either fillet, rump or sirloin)
2–3 tablespoons oil
salt and pepper

Rinse steaks quickly under cold running water and dry thoroughly with absorbent kitchen paper. Heat the oil in a frying pan and fry steaks on both sides. The exact time will vary according to taste. Season well. Serve with Corn salad (see page 34).

NOTE Frying times for steaks weighing 200 g/7 oz each:

For a rare steak, fry on each side for 1–2 minutes over high heat to seal the outside and barely cook the inside.

For a medium-done steak, fry on each side for 3–4 minutes over medium heat, leaving the inside slightly pink.

For a well-done steak, fry on each side for 4–5 minutes over medium heat so the meat is cooked right through and no pink can be seen inside.

Hunter's steak (recipe above).

Sherry kebabs

(Illustrated opposite)

Preparation time: 10-15 minutes

12 (3.5-cm/1½-inch) cubes fillet steak, about 450 g/1 lb in weight
15 g/½ oz dripping or lard
1 level teaspoon curry powder
½ teaspoon paprika pepper
generous pinch each salt and pepper
3 tablespoons soy sauce
1 tablespoon Kirsch
1 tablespoon sherry
1–2 tablespoons tomato ketchup

Thread 3 beef cubes on to 4 skewers and fry in the dripping or lard over a high heat for 1 minute, turning constantly. Season with the curry powder, paprika, salt and pepper and continue frying and turning for a few minutes. Pour a little hot water into the frying pan and stir to loosen any sediment. Stir in the soy sauce, Kirsch and sherry and continue to stir until the sauce is heated through. Add the ketchup and continue stirring until the sauce thickens. Pour the sauce into a sauce-boat and arrange the skewers on a plate. Serve the meat with green and tomato salads.

Maryland veal steak

Preparation time: 10-15 minutes

2 tablespoons oil
4 (150-g/5-oz) veal steaks
generous pinch each salt, pepper and paprika pepper
175 g/6 oz canned sweet corn kernels, drained
4 tablespoons single cream

Heat the oil in a frying pan and fry the veal for 4 minutes on each side. Season with a little salt, pepper and paprika and set aside on to a plate to keep hot. In a small saucepan, over gentle heat, warm the sweet corn with the cream and any remaining fat from the frying pan. Season with salt and paprika and pour over the steaks to serve. Serve with Rice with mushrooms (see page 25).

Above: Sherry kebabs (recipe above); *Below:* Veal steaks in soy sauce (recipe above right); Apricot cream (page 56).

Veal steaks in soy sauce

(Illustrated opposite)

Preparation time: 10-15 minutes

4 (100-g/4-oz) veal steaks
2 tablespoons oil
2 teaspoons soy sauce
salt and freshly ground pepper
1 (142-ml/5-fl oz) carton natural yogurt
1 tablespoon chopped parsley

Briefly rinse veal steaks under cold running water and dry with absorbent kitchen paper. Heat the oil in a frying pan and fry the steaks with the soy sauce for 5–6 minutes on each side. Sprinkle with salt and set aside on a serving dish to keep warm. Mix together with the fat remaining in the pan, the yogurt, pepper and parsley and heat through. Pour over the steaks to serve. Serve with bread or potato chips.

Escalopes of veal with tomatoes

Preparation time: 10-15 minutes

1 tablespoon oil
4 (75-g/3-oz) veal escalopes
½ teaspoon salt
freshly ground pepper
4 tomatoes

Heat the oil in a frying pan and fry the escalopes on one side only for 4 minutes. Mix the salt with a little pepper and sprinkle some over the veal. Turn the escalopes and cook on the other side for a further 4 minutes. Rinse and dry the tomatoes and cut each one in half. Sprinkle with a little more salt and pepper and fry for 4 minutes with the veal. Adjust the seasoning before serving.

Savoury cheese hamburgers.

Savoury cheese hamburgers

(Illustrated above)

Preparation time: 15-25 minutes

675 g/1 lb 8 oz minced beef
salt and pepper
1 egg, lightly beaten
50–75 g/2–3 oz Cheddar cheese, diced
1 tablespoon oil

Put the minced beef in a bowl, season well and bind with the beaten egg. Add the diced cheese and mix well. Divide the beef into 4 equal portions and shape each into a hamburger. Heat the oil in a frying pan and fry the hamburgers for about 4–5 minutes on each side, according to how well done you like your meat. Serve with cooked green vegetables and instant mashed potato.

Mexican meatballs

Preparation time: 15-25 minutes

450 g/1 lb minced beef
1 egg, lightly beaten
salt and pepper
2 tablespoons oil
25 g/1 oz butter
1 jar mini corn cobs (see note)
1 (184-g/6½-oz) can pimientos
2 tablespoons single cream
1 level teaspoon paprika pepper
pinch each salt and pepper
1 tablespoon tomato ketchup

In a bowl, combine the beef with the egg and seasoning to taste. Using a spoon, divide the beef into equal portions, rolling each into a ball about the size of an egg. Heat the oil in a large frying pan and cook the meatballs for about 8 minutes, turning frequently so they brown evenly. Set aside and keep hot. Melt the butter in a flameproof casserole and add the mini corn cobs, with a little of the liquid from the can, and heat through, stirring gently. Drain and chop the pimientos and add to the corn cobs in the casserole. Stir together the remaining ingredients, add them to the corn and allow to heat through. Serve the meatballs on a warmed dish or 4 individual plates and cover with the corn mixture. Serve with Continental potato salad (see page 32) or wholewheat bread.

NOTE If mini corn cobs are not readily available, substitute 1 (340-g/12-oz) can sweet corn kernels.

Fillet steak with parsley potatoes

Preparation time: 15-25 minutes

675 g/1½ lb small new potatoes, cooked in their skins
1 tablespoon dripping or oil
1 teaspoon salt
1 tablespoon chopped parsley
4 (150-g/5-oz) fillet steaks
1 tablespoon oil
½ teaspoon paprika pepper
4 tomatoes
15 g/½ oz butter
pepper

Carefully peel the cooked potatoes and cut any larger ones in half. Heat the dripping or oil in a frying pan, toss the potato in it and sprinkle with half the salt. Cover the pan and leave the potato to heat through over a low heat, stirring from time to time to prevent them from sticking. Add the parsley and toss to coat the potato. Keep warm. Rinse the meat under cold running water and dry with absorbent kitchen paper. Heat the oil in another frying pan and fry the fillets for 6 minutes on each side. Season with the remaining salt and the paprika, transfer to a dish and keep warm. Wash the tomatoes and, with a sharp knife, make a few incisions on the underside to prevent them splitting when cooked. Heat the butter in the juices remaining in the frying pan and add the tomatoes, season with pepper, cover and heat through over medium heat. Serve the fillets with tomatoes and parsley potatoes. Serve with Green salad with mayonnaise sauce (see page 36).

Madeira ragoût

Preparation time: 15-25 minutes

1 pickled cucumber
75 g/3 oz pickled beetroot
75 g/3 oz canned button mushrooms
1 tablespoon capers
250 g/9 oz fillet steak
200 g/7 oz lean pork
15 g/½ oz butter
1 tablespoon oil
½ teaspoon salt
¼ teaspoon pepper
½ teaspoon paprika pepper
4 tablespoons single cream
1 glass Madeira

Slice the cucumber and beetroot into thin strips. Drain and slice the mushrooms. Drain the capers. Remove any fat from the meat and cut into neat, even-sized pieces. Heat the butter and oil in a frying pan and gradually add the meat, shaking the pan and turning the meat until it is cooked and browned. Season with salt, pepper and paprika. Add the cucumber, beetroot, mushrooms and capers, mix well and cook over a low heat for about 10 minutes. Remove the pan from the heat, stir in the cream and Madeira. Serve immediately with bread and Chicory salad (see page 35).

NOTE If you have no Madeira, use sherry instead. A medium or dry sherry would be best.

Spicy pork cutlets

(Illustrated opposite)

Preparation time: 15-25 minutes

4 (100-g/4-oz) pork cutlets
½ teaspoon salt
¼ teaspoon pepper
1 tablespoon plain flour
1 egg, beaten
50 g/2 oz dry breadcrumbs
2 tablespoons oil
1 (213-g/7½-oz) can button mushrooms
4 tablespoons bought ready-made barbecue sauce
2 tomatoes
50 g/2 oz Edam cheese, sliced
4 slices bread

Set the oven at hot (230 C, 450 F, Gas Mark 8), or heat a grill to maximum. Season the pork with salt and pepper, toss in the flour, then dip in beaten egg and finally in the breadcrumbs. Heat the oil in a frying pan and fry the cutlets for about 6 minutes on each side until crisp and brown. Drain and slice the mushrooms, put them into a saucepan with the barbecue sauce and gently heat through. Wash and halve the tomatoes. Set a tomato half on each cutlet and top with a slice of cheese. Lightly toast the bread on both sides and place a cutlet on each slice. Place on a baking tray and bake in the oven or under the grill until the cheese begins to melt. Pour the sauce over the cutlets and serve with Green salad with mayonnaise sauce (see page 36) and potato chips.

Savoury pork or chicken omelette

(Illustrated opposite)

Preparation time: 15-25 minutes

½ (450-g/1-lb) jar sauerkraut
200 g/7 oz smoked pork or chicken
1 tablespoon lard
1 small onion, chopped
4 eggs
1 teaspoon salt
2 tablespoons whisky
300 ml/½ pint water
50 g/2 oz plain flour
2 tablespoons dripping
300 ml/½ pint instant white sauce made-up following the instructions on the packet
4 tablespoons tomato purée
25 g/1 oz grated cheese

Drain the sauerkraut and separate with a fork. Dice the pork or chicken. Melt the lard in a large frying pan and fry the onion until crisp. Add the sauerkraut and meat and stir well. Cover and simmer for 15 minutes.

In a bowl, whisk the eggs with the salt, whisky and water, then slowly stir in the flour to make a batter. In another frying pan, heat the dripping and make 4 pancake-like omelettes with the batter (see Spinach pancakes page 53). Transfer to a dish to keep them warm.

To the made-up white sauce, add the tomato purée and cheese and heat through. Arrange the omelettes on 4 individual plates, fill each with the sauerkraut mixture and fold over. Serve with the tomato and cheese sauce.

Opposite above: Spicy pork cutlets (recipe above left); *Below:* Savoury chicken omelette (recipe above).

Veal cutlets Rosemarino.

Veal cutlets Rosemarino

(Illustrated above)

Preparation time: 15-25 minutes

150 ml/$\frac{1}{4}$ pint water
4 large tomatoes
350 g/12 oz frozen peas
1 teaspoon salt
15 g/$\frac{1}{2}$ oz butter
4 (150-g/5-oz) best end veal cutlets
2 tablespoons oil
pepper
4 small sprigs fresh rosemary

Bring the water to the boil in a saucepan. Make a few incisions at the bottom of each tomato with a sharp knife. Pour over boiling water and leave for 2 minutes. Put the frozen peas into another saucepan with some of the salt and 2 tablespoons water, cover and cook over a low heat. Drain and peel the tomatoes, cut off the top third and carefully hollow out the flesh. Melt the butter in a frying pan, add the tomatoes, cover and simmer gently for 5 minutes. Rinse the cutlets under cold running water and dry with absorbent kitchen paper. Heat the oil in a frying pan and fry the cutlets for 6 minutes on each side. Season with salt and pepper. Arrange the cutlets on a warm dish, garnish with rosemary (if fresh is not available, use $\frac{1}{2}$ teaspoon dried). Drain the peas and use to fill the hollowed-out tomatoes. Serve the cutlets with the stuffed tomatoes arranged on one side and with Parsley potatoes (see page 19) as an accompaniment.

Variations

Coat the veal cutlets in beaten egg then dry breadcrumbs, or first in seasoned flour, then beaten egg and dry breadcrumbs mixed with grated Parmesan cheese. Fry the cutlets as above and serve with herb butter.

For a simple dish that is suitable for entertaining, serve the breadcrumbed veal cutlets with buttered peas tossed with strips of ham.

Chicken liver ragoût

Preparation time: 15-25 minutes

1 (425-g/15-oz) can peeled tomatoes
200 g/7 oz canned button mushrooms
50 g/2 oz butter
1 small onion, chopped
450 g/1 lb chicken livers
1 level teaspoon cornflour
½ teaspoon salt
¼ teaspoon pepper
100 ml/4 fl oz single cream
3 tablespoons chopped parsley

Thoroughly drain the tomatoes and mushrooms, reserving the liquid from both cans. Make the liquid up to 600 ml/1 pint with a little water. Melt the butter in a flameproof casserole and gently fry the onion. Add the chicken livers and fry gently on all sides for about 4 minutes. Mix the cornflour with a little of the reserved liquid and season well. Add the remaining liquid, the tomatoes, mushrooms and cornflour to the liver, stir to mix and bring to the boil, stirring constantly. Allow to boil gently for 1 minute before taking the ragoût off the heat. Stir in the cream and sprinkle with parsley to serve.

Spring chicken

Preparation time: 15-25 minutes

4 chicken breasts
2 teaspoons lemon juice
2 tablespoons oil
12 cocktail onions
200 g/7 oz canned button mushrooms, drained
1 (227-g/8-oz) can peeled tomatoes, drained
generous pinch each salt, pepper and dried marjoram or oregano
4 tablespoons tomato ketchup

Place the chicken on a plate and sprinkle with the lemon juice. Heat the oil in a frying pan and fry the onions until just browned. Add the chicken breasts and fry over low heat for 6–7 minutes on each side. Arrange the mushrooms and tomatoes on top of the chicken, cover and allow to heat through. Season the ketchup and pour it over the chicken. Serve with mashed potato or buttered noodles and a crisp green salad.

NOTE Rashers of streaky bacon, derinded and fried until crisp can be added with the onions.

Chicken paprika

(Illustrated on page 24)

Preparation time: 15-25 minutes

1 onion
25 g/1 oz butter
15 g/½ oz plain flour
1 (397-g/14-oz) can peeled tomatoes
2 (184-g/6½-oz) can pimientos, drained
225 g/8 oz frozen peas
1 (1.5-kg/3-lb) cooked chicken
¼ teaspoon salt
generous pinch each salt and paprika pepper
150 ml/¼ pint soured cream

Peel and chop the onion. Melt the butter in a flameproof casserole and lightly fry the onion, stirring so that it does not stick. Dust with the flour while stirring lightly. Pour in the tomatoes with the juice from the can and mix well while it is heating through. Add the pimientos and frozen peas, cover the casserole and cook gently over a low heat. Cut the chicken into individual portions and heat up thoroughly in the sauce. Mix together the seasonings and soured cream and stir into the sauce just before serving. Serve with Fruit and nut salad (see page 38) and follow with Orange surprise (see page 56).

Rice, pasta and potatoes

Rice accompaniments

The following are useful ways to use up leftover ready-cooked rice.

Preparation time: 10-15 minutes

Rice with mushrooms

Thinly slice 75–100 g/3–4 oz mushrooms and fry gently in 25 g/1 oz butter. Add 575 g/1¼ lb cooked rice (made up from 190 g/6½ oz uncooked rice following the instructions on the packet). Cover and allow the rice to heat through. Stir in 1 tablespoon of chopped parsley before serving.

Curried rice

Reheat 575 g/1¼ lb cooked rice (see above recipe for uncooked quantity) in a covered colander over steam, if necessary. Melt 15 g/½ oz butter in a pan, add the rice and 1–2 teaspoons of curry powder to taste. Mix well and serve.

Risi Pisi

(An Italian rice dish.) Reheat 575 g/1¼ lb cooked rice (see Rice with mushrooms for uncooked quantity) in a covered colander over steam, if necessary. Melt 15 g/½ oz butter in a pan, add 100 g/4 oz frozen peas, cover and allow to heat through for about 6 minutes. Add the peas to the rice and mix well before serving.

Tomato rice

Reheat 575 g/1¼ lb cooked rice (see Rice with mushrooms for uncooked quantity) in a covered colander over steam, if necessary. Melt 15 g/½ oz butter in a saucepan, heat 3–4 tablespoons tomato purée in the butter and add the rice. Mix well and season before serving.

Opposite above: Ravioli with mixed vegetables (page 28); *Below:* Chicken paprika (page 23).

Hungarian savoury rice

Preparation time: 10-15 minutes

---

1 tablespoon oil
350 g/12 oz minced beef
1 small onion
100 ml/4 fl oz stock, made up with stock cubes if necessary
575 g/1¼ lb cooked rice (see note)
1 (425-g/15-oz) can peeled tomatoes
½ (340-g/12-oz) can asparagus tips
1 (213-g/7½-oz) can button mushrooms
pinch each salt, pepper and paprika pepper
2 tablespoons chopped parsley

Heat the oil in a flameproof casserole and lightly fry the meat until evenly browned. Peel and chop the onion and add it to the meat. Bring the stock to the boil in a saucepan, then stir it into the meat with the rice and tomatoes with their juice. Mix well. Drain the asparagus and the mushrooms and add them to the rice mixture. Season to taste, add the paprika and heat through. Serve hot, garnished with the chopped parsley. Finish with fruit yogurt.

NOTE 575 g/1¼ lb cooked rice is made up using 190 g/6½ oz uncooked rice following the instructions on the packet.

Rice salad

Preparation time: 10-15 minutes

2 small pickled cucumbers
1 banana
50 g/2 oz canned mandarin oranges
275 g/10 oz canned or frozen peeled prawns, thawed
450 g/1 lb cooked rice (see note)
1 (142-ml/5-fl oz) carton natural yogurt
2 tablespoons mayonnaise
few drops lemon juice
½ teaspoon salt
1 level teaspoon curry powder
generous pinch of castor sugar

Dice the cucumbers; peel and dice the banana. Drain and chop the mandarin oranges, reserving the juice. Drain the prawns and rinse under cold running water. Chop and mix together with cucumber, banana, mandarin oranges and cooked rice. Mix together yogurt, mayonnaise, 2 tablespoons of the reserved juice, lemon juice, salt, curry powder and sugar and fold into the rice mixture, making sure it is evenly distributed. Turn into a dish and serve with a crisp green salad.

NOTE For 450 g/1 lb cooked rice, use 150 g/5½ oz uncooked. Follow the instructions on the packet, then allow to cool before using for salad dishes.

Paprika rice

(Illustrated opposite)

Preparation time: 15-25 minutes

3 green peppers
2 tablespoons oil
400 g/14 oz minced beef
1 small onion
100 ml/4 fl oz stock, made with a stock cube if necessary
575 g/1¼ lb cooked rice (see note)
25 g/1 oz cheese, grated
½ teaspoon salt
½ teaspoon paprika pepper

Cut each pepper in half, deseed and remove and discard the core. Wash the flesh and cut into thin strips. Heat the oil in a large saucepan and fry the pepper for about 5 minutes, stirring all the time to prevent scorching. Add the meat and the peeled and chopped onion, and fry until the meat is evenly cooked and the onion transparent. Bring the stock to the boil in a small saucepan and add it to the meat mixture. Stir in the rice and cheese. Season with salt and paprika, mix well, cover and simmer over medium heat for about 5 minutes until the rice is heated through.

NOTE For 575 g/1¼ lb cooked rice, use 190 g/6½ oz uncooked. Follow the instructions on the packet, then allow to cool.

Curried rice with banana rolls

Preparation time: 15-25 minutes

225 g/8 oz rice
4 firm bananas
2 tablespoons dripping
1 teaspoon paprika pepper
4 (50-g/2-oz) slices lean cooked ham
4 tablespoons curry paste

Cook the rice following the instructions on the packet. Drain and briefly rinse in a colander or sieve. Meanwhile, peel the bananas and slice in half, lengthwise. Set the oven at hot (230 C, 450 F, Gas Mark 8). Melt the dripping in a frying pan, sprinkle the banana slices with paprika and gently fry them over low heat for about 1 minute. Put 2 banana halves together and wrap each pair in a slice of ham. Stir the curry paste into the remaining dripping in the pan and when it is well mixed, add the cooked rice, stirring to mix it in well. Place the curried rice in an ovenproof dish, arrange the ham and banana rolls on top and place in the oven or under a pre-heated hot grill to heat through for 5 minutes. Serve with Simple tomato salad (see page 34) or Green salad with mayonnaise sauce (see page 36).

Opposite above: Paprika rice (recipe left); *Centre:* Sweet and sour potato salad (page 32) served with fried fish fingers.

Cooking pasta

There are many different types of pasta available on the market, such as flat noodles, straight macaroni, elbow macaroni, spaghetti and shell and bow shapes that present many possibilities when making the various pasta dishes. Pasta is a useful storecupboard item for unexpected guests.

Whatever shape of pasta is used, it is important to follow the cooking instructions on the packet.

Here are some useful extra hints

Remember that for a main course, you should allow 75–100 g/3–4 oz pasta per person.

Cook all pasta in plenty of boiling salted water, rinse briefly under cold running water and drain well before serving. A teaspoon of oil in the cooking water will help prevent it sticking together while cooking.

Ravioli with mixed vegetables

(Illustrated on page 24)

Preparation time: 10-15 minutes

1 (440-g/15-oz) can ravioli in tomato sauce
400 g/14 oz canned mixed vegetables, drained
150 ml/¼ pint soured cream
100 g/4 oz cheese, grated
3 tablespoons chopped parsley
25 g/1 oz cold butter, flaked

Set the oven at hot (230 C, 450 F, Gas Mark 8). Fill an ovenproof dish with alternate layers of ravioli and vegetables, ending with ravioli. Pour the soured cream over the top and sprinkle with the cheese, then 2 tablespoons of the parsley. Dot with flaked butter and cook for 10 minutes or until the top is golden brown. Sprinkle with the rest of the chopped parsley and serve with Fruit and nut salad (see page 38) and follow with Orange surprise (see page 56).

Ravioli casserole

Preparation time: 10-15 minutes

1 (440-g/15-oz) can ravioli in tomato sauce
450 g/1 lb frozen peas
350 g/12 oz cooked ham
4 tablespoons dry breadcrumbs
6 tablespoons grated cheese
25 g/1 oz cold butter, flaked

Set the oven at hot (230 C, 450 F, Gas Mark 8). Open the ravioli, leave the lid lying loose on top and stand the can in a saucepan of boiling water to heat through. In another saucepan, place the peas with 2 tablespoons salted water and allow to cook for 3 minutes over low heat. Dice the ham. Lightly grease an ovenproof casserole. Add half the ravioli, the peas, then a layer of ham and finish with the remaining ravioli. Mix the breadcrumbs with the cheese and sprinkle over the ravioli. Dot the top with the flaked butter and bake in the oven for 8 minutes or until cooked through. Serve with Corn salad (see page 34) or Radish and apple salad (see page 36).

Mussel ragoût

Preparation time: 15-25 minutes

200 g/7 oz shell pasta
1 teaspoon salt
1 onion
400 g/14 oz canned mussels in brine
2 tablespoons oil
1 (397-g/14-oz) can peeled tomatoes, drained
generous pinch each salt, pepper and garlic salt

Cook the pasta with the salt following the instructions on the packet. Peel and dice the onion. Drain the mussels and reserve the liquid. In a frying pan, heat the oil and lightly fry the onion, tomatoes, mussels and a little of the reserved liquid. Cover and allow to warm through over low heat for 10 minutes. Meanwhile, drain the cooked pasta, and mix in the mussels and tomato mixture, seasoning to taste with salt, pepper and garlic salt. Serve immediately.

Chicken casserole with tomatoes.

Chicken casserole with tomatoes

(Illustrated above)

Preparation time: 15-25 minutes

200 g/7 oz spaghetti
1 teaspoon salt
1 (1.5-kg/3-lb) cooked chicken
1 onion
1 clove garlic
1 (184-g/6½-oz) can pimientos
1 (227-g/8-oz) can peeled tomatoes
2 tablespoons oil
150 ml/¼ pint red wine
2 tablespoons chopped parsley

Cook the spaghetti in boiling salted water following the instructions on the packet. Remove the meat from the chicken, discarding the bones and skin (save these for making stock), and chop the meat into small pieces. Peel and dice the onion. Peel, dice and crush the garlic. Drain the pimientos and tomatoes and chop in thin slices. Heat the oil in a flameproof casserole and lightly fry the onion and garlic, stirring continuously. Add the pimiento and tomato and continue to fry. Add the chicken and wine, cover the pan and heat through over low heat. Drain the spaghetti and rinse briefly under cold running water before adding to the chicken in the casserole. Toss and allow to heat through before garnishing with the parsley to serve.

NOTE To make a substantial lunch or supper, serve a simple vegetable or chicken and vegetable soup as a first course, then follow with the chicken casserole.

Spaghetti bolognese

(Illustrated opposite)

Preparation time: 15-25 minutes

350 g/12 oz spaghetti
1½ teaspoons salt
3 tablespoons olive oil
1 small onion, peeled and chopped
400 g/14 oz minced beef
2 tablespoons tomato purée
1 (227-g/8-oz) can peeled tomatoes, drained
¼ teaspoon pepper
1 teaspoon paprika pepper
100 ml/4 fl oz white wine
100 g/4 oz Parmesan cheese, grated

Cook the spaghetti with 1 teaspoon of the salt in boiling water, following the instructions on the packet. Heat the oil in a flameproof casserole and fry the onion. Add the meat and stir until evenly cooked and browned. Add the tomato purée and tomatoes and stir until thoroughly heated. Add the seasoning and wine, mix well, then cover and simmer for 10 minutes. Drain the spaghetti in a colander or sieve and rinse quickly under cold running water. Serve on a large dish with the sauce poured over and with the grated cheese handed separately. Accompany with a crisp green salad.

Ham noodles

Preparation time: 15-25 minutes

200 g/7 oz noodles
15–25 g/½–1 oz butter
1 onion, peeled and chopped
200 g/7 oz cooked ham, cut in strips
100 ml/4 fl oz soured cream
1 egg

Cook the noodles following the instructions on the packet and quickly rinse under cold running water. Drain well. Melt the butter in a frying pan and fry the onion and ham. Add the noodles to the onion mixture and heat through. Whisk together the soured cream and egg, pour over the hot noodles and toss to allow the egg to set. Serve with a crisp green salad.

Spaghetti bolognese.

Potato accompaniments

Here are some simple but tasty ways to serve mashed potato. Use 1 (127-g/4½ oz) packet instant mashed potato for each dish.

Preparation time: 5-10 minutes

Puréed potato with bacon

In a frying pan, lightly fry 50–100 g/2–4 oz chopped streaky bacon and 1 peeled and chopped onion. Make up the mashed potato following the instructions on the packet and mix together with the bacon and onion. Season to taste.

Puréed potato with sauerkraut

Drain and chop 275 g/10 oz sauerkraut and mix in 2–3 tablespoons unsweetened apple juice. Stir into the made-up mashed potato. Melt 15 g/½ oz butter in a saucepan and add the potato. Heat through over gentle heat, stirring continuously.

Potato purée with horseradish

Peel, core and grate 1 large dessert apple and mix together with 2–3 tablespoons grated horseradish or horseradish cream (according to taste). Mix with the made-up mashed potato. Melt 15 g/½ oz butter in a saucepan, add the potato and heat through over gentle heat, stirring continuously.

The following recipes make the most of leftover cooked whole potatoes. Estimate 175–225 g/6–8 oz potatoes per person. The recipes will serve 4 as substantial accompaniments or buffet dishes.

Lyonnaise potatoes

In a frying pan, melt 25 g/1 oz butter. Peel and dice 1 onion and lightly fry. Peel and slice the potatoes, sprinkle with salt and fry over a low heat on both sides until golden brown.

Sauté potatoes

In a frying pan, melt 40 g/1½ oz butter. Peel and slice the potatoes, season with salt and pepper and fry on both sides until golden brown.

Sauté potatoes with bacon

Prepare the potatoes as for Sauté potatoes, but fry with 100 g/4 oz chopped streaky bacon.

Variation

Add 1–2 lightly beaten eggs to the mixture, sprinkle with caraway seeds and stir until set.

Continental potato salad

Peel and slice the potatoes and pour over 175 ml/6 fl oz hot stock. Stir in 2 tablespoons chopped parsley, 1 tablespoon vinegar, 2 tablespoons oil and season with salt and pepper. Add sliced Frankfurters or sliced Mortadella or Continental ham sausage, or any chopped leftover meat. Mix together thoroughly and drain before serving warm or cold.

Herring and potato salad

Peel and slice the potatoes and season with salt and pepper. Add 225 g/8 oz diced cooked beetroot and 300 g/11 oz ready-made herring salad from a local delicatessen. Mix together well.

Sweet and sour potato salad

(Illustrated on page 27)

Peel and slice the potatoes and season with salt and pepper. Core and dice 1 apple, dice 1 pickled cucumber and 1 onion. Combine all these ingredients and add 1 tablespoon wine vinegar, 100 ml/4 fl oz mayonnaise, ½ teaspoon sugar and a generous pinch of dried marjoram, according to taste. Toss the salad with a few drops of lemon juice. This is particularly good served with fried fish fingers.

Savoury potato croquettes

(Illustrated opposite)

Preparation time: 10-15 minutes

1 (127-g/4½-oz) packet instant mashed potato
4 tablespoons grated Parmesan cheese
8 streaky bacon rashers
2 tablespoons dripping
1 Spanish onion
1 (227-g/8-oz) can peeled tomatoes, drained
2 tablespoons chopped parsley
1 tablespoon oil
1 tablespoon wine vinegar
175–225 g/6–8 oz cottage cheese
salt and pepper

Make up the instant mashed potato following the instructions on the packet. Mix in the Parmesan cheese and leave to stand for 5 minutes. In a frying pan, fry the bacon in its own fat until crisp and brown. Remove the bacon and heat the dripping in the same frying pan. Form the potato into 8 croquettes and fry in the dripping over low heat until crisp and brown on both sides. Peel and dice the onion; chop the tomatoes. Mix together the onion, tomato, parsley, oil, vinegar and cottage cheese, season to taste and serve with the croquettes in a separate bowl. Serve each potato croquette topped with a bacon rasher.

Savoury potato croquettes.

Destilacion
ESPECIAL

Salads

Corn salad

(Illustrated below)

Preparation time: 5-10 minutes

1 large carrot
2 apples
1 (198-g/7-oz) can sweet corn kernels
2 teaspoons lemon juice
½ teaspoon sugar
1 red pepper, deseeded and cut into strips
½ (142-ml/5-fl oz) carton natural yogurt
1 tablespoon oil
½ teaspoon salt
¼ teaspoon paprika pepper

Peel and wash the carrot, peel and core the apples and grate both. Drain the corn. Mix together the carrot, apple, corn, lemon juice, sugar and red pepper. Mix together the yogurt, oil, salt and paprika and fold the dressing into the salad. Serve in 1 large or 4 individual bowls with Classic steak (see page 15).

Corn salad.

Cucumber salad

Preparation time: 5-10 minutes

1 small cucumber
1 (142-ml/5-fl oz) carton natural yogurt
salt and pepper

Wash, dry and finely slice the unpeeled cucumber into a bowl. Combine with yogurt and salt and pepper to taste and serve immediately.

Simple tomato salad

Preparation time: 5-10 minutes

4 large tomatoes
1 onion
¼ teaspoon each salt and pepper
1 tablespoon oil
1 teaspoon lemon juice

Wash and dry the tomatoes and slice thinly. Peel and dice the onion. Arrange the tomato slices on a plate and sprinkle with salt, pepper and diced onion. Mix together the oil and lemon juice and pour evenly over the salad before serving.

Chicory salad

Preparation time: 5-10 minutes

2 heads chicory
2 bunches radishes
½ cucumber
1 tablespoon oil
1 tablespoon white wine vinegar
1 tablespoon apple juice
1 tablespoon orange juice
½ teaspoon salt
¼ teaspoon pepper
2 tablespoons chopped parsley

Cut off the hard base stems of the chicory, halve the heads and wash and drain well before slicing. Wash, top and tail, then slice the radishes; wash and slice the unpeeled cucumber. Mix together the oil, vinegar, apple and orange juice, salt and pepper and stir into the salad ingredients. Sprinkle over the chopped parsley and toss lightly before serving.

Haricot and tomato salad

Preparation time: 5-10 minutes

200-g/7-oz canned haricot beans
1 (227-g/8-oz) can peeled tomatoes
1 large dessert apple
100 g/4 oz celeriac, sliced
1 tablespoon wine vinegar
2 tablespoons oil
generous pinch each salt, garlic salt and pepper
few drops Worcestershire sauce (see note)
2 tablespoons chopped parsley

Drain the beans. Drain the tomatoes and chop them. Peel, core and dice the apple. Mix these ingredients with the sliced celeriac. Mix the vinegar, oil, salt, garlic salt, pepper and Worcestershire sauce and gently stir this dressing into the salad ingredients. Put the salad into a bowl, toss and sprinkle with parsley to serve.

NOTE It is possible to substitute 1 medium onion, chopped, for the Worcestershire sauce.

Haricot bean salad

Preparation time: 5-10 minutes

200-g/7-oz canned haricot beans
1 (184-g/6½-oz) can pimientos
100 g/4 oz celeriac, grated
90 g/3½ oz Cheddar cheese, diced
4 tablespoons mayonnaise
1 teaspoon wine vinegar
½ teaspoon mustard
dash Worcestershire sauce
¼ teaspoon salt

Drain the haricot beans. Drain and chop the pimientos and mix together with the beans, celeriac and cheese. Combine the mayonnaise with the vinegar, mustard, Worcestershire sauce and salt. Fold the dressing into the salad and toss well before serving. Serve with wholewheat bread.

Cucumber fruit salad

Preparation time: 5-10 minutes

200 g/7 oz pickled cucumbers, drained
2 dessert apples
2 bananas
2 teaspoons lemon juice
1 small lettuce
2 tomatoes
50 g/2 oz curd cheese
2 tablespoons mayonnaise
1 tablespoon finely-chopped hazelnuts

Dice the cucumbers. Peel, core and dice the apples; peel and dice the bananas. Mix the fruit and sprinkle with the lemon juice to prevent discoloration. Separate the lettuce, removing any coarse outer leaves or hard stalk and wash and dry the rest. Tear into small pieces and add to the fruit. Wash, dry and dice the tomatoes and add these also. Mix together the curd cheese and mayonnaise and stir into the salad ingredients. Serve sprinkled with the hazelnuts.

Radish and apple salad

Preparation time: 5-10 minutes

small bunch radishes
2 small dessert apples
2 teaspoons lemon juice
1 level teaspoon castor sugar
generous pinch each salt and pepper
1 tablespoon wine vinegar
1 tablespoon oil
½ teaspoon mustard
2 tablespoons chopped parsley

Wash, trim and thinly slice the radishes. Peel, core and grate the apples. Mix together with the lemon juice, sugar, seasoning, vinegar, oil and mustard. Toss, and sprinkle with parsley.

Green salad with mayonnaise sauce

Preparation time: 5-10 minutes

1 crisp lettuce
2 tablespoons mayonnaise
2 tablespoons single cream
2 tablespoons wine vinegar
¼ teaspoon each sugar and salt
½ teaspoon paprika pepper

Separate the lettuce, removing any coarse outer leaves or hard stalk and tear the rest into small pieces. Wash under cold running water and drain. Mix together the remaining ingredients and toss gently with the lettuce just before serving.

Variations

Substitute lemon, orange or pineapple juice for the mayonnaise and continue as above.

Alternatively, make a dressing with 75 g/3 oz crumbled Danish blue cheese mixed with 6 tablespoons single cream, 1 teaspoon lemon juice and a generous pinch of pepper.

South sea salad

(Illustrated opposite)

Preparation time: 10-15 minutes

1 grapefruit
1 (198-g/7-oz) can shrimps
4 canned pineapple rings
50 g/2 oz button mushrooms
½ medium cucumber
225 g/8 oz artichoke bottoms
100 ml/4 fl oz single cream
1 teaspoon grated horseradish
1 tablespoon tomato ketchup
generous pinch each salt and pepper

Peel and dice the grapefruit flesh removing any pips. Drain and rinse the shrimps under cold running water. Drain the pineapple and dice; slice the mushrooms. Peel the cucumber, cut it in half lengthwise, then remove the seeds and slice. Drain and rinse the artichoke bottoms and cut each in half. Mix together the cream, horseradish, ketchup and seasoning. Toss all the salad ingredients together and divide into 4 individual bowls. Pour some dressing over each to serve.

Smoked mackerel salad

Preparation time: 10-15 minutes

1 green pepper
1 dessert apple
225 g/8 oz celeriac, peeled
1 pickled cucumber
200 g/7 oz smoked mackerel
½ teaspoon curry powder
100 ml/4 fl oz tomato ketchup

Halve and deseed the pepper, wash and cut it into thin strips. Peel and core the apple and cut it into strips. Chop the celeriac into thin slices, dice the cucumber and chop the fish into neat pieces. Combine these salad ingredients. Stir the curry powder into the ketchup and gently mix into the salad. Serve with French bread.

South sea salad (recipe above).

Fruit and nut salad

(Illustrated opposite)

Preparation time: 10-15 minutes

1 lettuce
2 tomatoes
1 banana
2 teaspoons lemon juice
100 g/4 oz celeriac, grated (optional)
3 canned pineapple rings
2 tablespoons oil
2 tablespoons finely-chopped mixed nuts
½ teaspoon salt
1 tablespoon chopped parsley
walnut half, to garnish

Separate the lettuce, removing any coarse outer leaves or hard stem. Tear into small pieces, wash under cold water and drain well. Wash and dry the tomatoes and cut each into 8. Peel and slice the banana and sprinkle with lemon juice to prevent discoloration. Mix together the lettuce, tomato, banana and grated celeriac, if used. Drain the pineapple and reserve the juice. Cut through the pineapple rings, horizontally, reserving one slice for garnish. Cut the remaining slices into small pieces and mix with the other salad ingredients. Mix together the oil, 2 tablespoons of the reserved pineapple juice, the nuts, salt and parsley and combine with salad. Place the reserved pineapple slice in the centre of the salad and garnish with the walnut.

Fish salad

(Illustrated opposite)

Preparation time: 10-15 minutes

4 rollmop herrings
150 g/5 oz canned tuna
1 small lettuce
6 tomatoes
3 eggs, hard-boiled
100 ml/4 fl oz buttermilk or soured cream
dash white wine vinegar
½ teaspoon sugar
pinch each salt, pepper and dried chervil

Briefly soak the herrings for a few minutes in cold water, then drain and cut into chunks. Drain the tuna reserving the oil. Remove any coarse outer leaves and hard stalk from the lettuce and wash and dry the rest. Rinse and dry the tomatoes and cut each into 8. Remove the shell from the eggs and chop. Whisk together the remaining ingredients and the reserved tuna oil. Lightly toss all the salad ingredients in the dressing and serve with jacket potatoes or Continental potato salad (see page 32).

Yogurt pea salad

Preparation time: 15-25 minutes

250 ml/8 fl oz water
generous pinch salt
300 g/11 oz frozen peas
100 g/4 oz lean cooked ham
2 eggs, hard-boiled
leaves of lemon balm, if available
1 tablespoon lemon juice
1 teaspoon castor sugar
pinch white pepper
1 (142-ml/5-fl oz) carton natural yogurt
2 tablespoons chopped parsley

Bring the water to the boil with the salt in a saucepan, add the peas, cover and simmer over gentle heat until cooked. Meanwhile, cut the ham into strips. Remove the shell from the eggs and cut each one into 8. Wash and chop some lemon balm, if available. Drain the peas and mix together with egg and ham.

Mix together the lemon juice, sugar, pepper and yogurt and stir gently into the salad ingredients. Garnish with parsley and lemon balm, if available, and serve with toast.

Opposite above: Fruit and nut salad (recipe above left); *Below:* Fish salad (recipe left).

Snacks

Fried egg snack

Preparation time: 5-10 minutes

1 tablespoon oil
8 streaky bacon rashers
8 eggs
salt and pepper
4 slices wholewheat bread

Heat the oil in a frying pan and fry the bacon until crisp. Break an egg on to each bacon rasher and fry until the egg is cooked. Season with salt and pepper. Arrange 2 eggs and 2 bacon rashers on each slice of bread for serving.

Spicy egg on toast

Preparation time: 5-10 minutes

4 lettuce leaves
4 slices wholewheat bread
1 tablespoon sandwich spread
4 eggs, hard-boiled
50 g/2 oz curd cheese
1–2 teaspoons grated horseradish or horseradish cream
pinch each salt and pepper
dash Worcestershire sauce
tomato ketchup (optional)

Wash the lettuce leaves and pat dry. Lightly toast the bread slices on both sides and spread with the sandwich spread. Remove the shell from the eggs and slice as thinly as possible. Place one lettuce leaf on each slice of toast and top with egg slices. Mix together the curd cheese, horseradish and seasoning. Add a dash of Worcestershire sauce and spoon this mixture over the egg slices. Swirl a little ketchup on each, if used.

Corned beef snack

Preparation time: 5-10 minutes

4 slices bread
2 tablespoons oil
4 slices corned beef
4 eggs
15 g/½ oz butter
pinch each salt and pepper
8 anchovy fillets
1 tablespoon capers

Lightly toast the bread on both sides. Heat the oil in a large frying pan and fry the corned beef slices on both sides. Place each slice of beef on one slice of toast and keep warm.

Meanwhile, fry the eggs in the butter and season with salt and pepper. Place a fried egg on each slice of corned beef and arrange anchovy fillets and capers on top. Serve with Simple tomato salad (see page 34).

Roast beef rolls

(Illustrated opposite)

Preparation time: 5-10 minutes

1 (432-g/15½-oz) jar pickled vegetables, such as cauliflower, cocktail onions and gherkins
8 slices cold roast beef

Chop half of the mixed pickles, and keep the rest whole. Divide the chopped mixture among the slices of roast beef and roll up. Serve with the remaining pickles on a separate dish and with French or wholewheat bread.

Roast beef rolls.

Toast tartare

Preparation time: 5-10 minutes

4 slices wholewheat bread
25 g/1 oz butter
1 teaspoon anchovy paste
400 g/14 oz very lean minced steak
2 egg yolks
¼ teaspoon each salt, pepper and paprika pepper
general dash Worcestershire sauce
4 canned anchovy fillets
a few capers

Lightly toast the bread on both sides. Cream the butter with anchovy paste and spread on the toast. In a bowl, mix together the steak, egg yolks, seasoning and Worcestershire sauce and divide among the buttered slices of toast. Garnish each with a rolled anchovy and a few capers.

Smoked ham on toast

Preparation time: 5-10 minutes

4 slices wholewheat bread
15 g/½ oz butter
1 small packet Petit Suisse medium-fat soft cheese
1 tablespoon single cream
¼ teaspoon curry paste
1 teaspoon ginger syrup from a jar of preserved ginger
generous pinch each salt and cayenne pepper
200 g/7 oz smoked ham, cut into strips
4 small pickled cucumbers

Lightly toast the bread on both sides and spread with the butter. Stir together the cheese, cream, curry paste, ginger syrup, salt and cayenne and spread on the slices of toast. Arrange the strips of ham on top, then cut each pickled cucumber into a fan shape and use to garnish each open sandwich.

Roast pork with pineapple

Preparation time: 5-10 minutes

8 large thin slices white bread
25 g/1 oz butter
4 thin slices cold roast pork
2 canned pineapple rings
1 tablespoon mayonnaise
1 teaspoon grated horseradish
½ teaspoon chilli powder, or to taste
1 teaspoon tomato ketchup

Spread the bread slices thinly with the butter and top 4 slices with a slice of pork. Slice the pineapple rings in half, horizontally, and top each pork slice. Mix together the mayonnaise, horseradish, chilli powder and ketchup and fill the centre of each pineapple ring with this mixture. Cover the sandwiches with the remaining bread slices.

Hawaiian toast

Preparation time: 5-10 minutes

4 large lettuce leaves
4 slices bread
15 g/½ oz butter
2 teaspoons grated horseradish
½ (225-g/8-oz) can crushed pineapple
2 tablespoons mayonnaise
1 teaspoon mango chutney
65 g/2½ oz curd cheese
2 level teaspoons paprika pepper
8 slices ham, cut to fit toast

Wash the lettuce leaves under cold running water and drain. Lightly toast the bread on both sides. Mix together the butter and horseradish and spread on the toast. Mix about 1 tablespoon of the crushed pineapple with the mayonnaise, chutney, curd cheese and paprika. On top of each piece of toast, place a lettuce leaf, a slice of ham and spread with the mayonnaise and cheese mixture; top with another ham slice and cover with the remaining crushed pineapple.

Left: Parma ham and melon sandwich (recipe below); *Right:* Tuna and shrimp sandwiches (page 48).

Parma ham and melon sandwich

(Illustrated above)

Preparation time: 5-10 minutes

4 large lettuce leaves
15 g/½ oz butter
4 slices wholewheat bread
8 slices Parma ham
½ honeydew melon
1 (312-g/11-oz) can mandarin segments, drained

Rinse the lettuce under cold running water and drain well. Butter the bread slices and place a lettuce leaf on each one with 2 slices of the ham. Remove the seeds from the melon, peel and cut the flesh into 8 wedges. Place 2 wedges on top of each open sandwich and garnish with segments of mandarin.

Sally's banana toast

Preparation time: 5-10 minutes

4 slices bread
2 bananas
1 teaspoon lemon juice
200 g/7 oz Cervelat sausage, cut in cubes (see note)
3 tablespoons mayonnaise
pinch each salt and paprika pepper
½ teaspoon mustard
1 teaspoon tomato ketchup
2 teaspoons chopped parsley

Lightly toast the slices of bread on both sides. Peel and chop the bananas and sprinkle with lemon juice to prevent discoloration. Combine the sausage with the bananas, mayonnaise, seasoning, mustard, ketchup and parsley. Spread over the slices of toast and serve with Chicory salad (see page 35).

NOTE Cervelat sausage is a sausage made of mixed pork, beef and bacon.

Welsh rarebit

Preparation time: 5-10 minutes

15 g/½ oz butter
4 slices bread
250 g/9 oz cheese, grated
4 tablespoons light beer or ale
2 teaspoons mild mustard
1 teaspoon Worcestershire sauce

Set the oven at hot (230 C, 450 F, Gas Mark 8) or heat a grill to maximum. In a frying pan, melt the butter and fry the slices of bread on one side only. Mix together the cheese, beer, mustard and Worcestershire sauce and spread the mixture on the unfried side of each slice of bread. Place in the oven or under the grill and heat through for a few minutes or until the top is bubbling and golden brown. Serve immediately.

Soft cheese and onion snack

Preparation time: 5-10 minutes

300–400 g/11–14 oz curd cheese
100–150 ml/4–5 fl oz milk or single cream
½ teaspoon salt
¼ teaspoon pepper
40 g/1½ oz chopped mixed herbs (see note)
1 small onion
wholewheat, rye or crispbread for serving

Combine the curd cheese, milk or cream, seasoning and herbs. Peel and dice the onion and gently stir into the cheese. Chill thoroughly and serve with wholewheat, rye or crispbread.

NOTE If fresh herbs are not available, use 1 tablespoon dried herbs and a little chopped fresh mustard and cress or parsley.

Variations

Curd cheese with cucumber Mix the same amount of curd cheese with the juice of 1 lemon, ½ an unpeeled, finely-chopped cucumber, a bunch of finely-chopped dill, parsley or chives and salt and celery salt to taste. Chill before serving.

Tomato and curd cheese Mix the same amount of curd cheese with 2 (227-g/8-oz) cans peeled tomatoes, drained and finely-chopped, 1 peeled and diced onion and salt and pepper to taste. Chill.

Paprika curd cheese Mix the same amount of curd cheese with 1 deseeded and diced red and green pepper, 1 peeled and finely-diced onion, and chopped chives, salt and paprika pepper to taste.

Ham curd cheese Mix the same amount of curd cheese with 100–150 ml/4–5 fl oz milk or single cream, 200 g/7 oz finely-chopped cooked ham, chopped parsley and salt to taste. Before serving, mix in 6 finely-chopped cocktail onions.

Sausage and cheese rolls

Preparation time: 5-10 minutes

8 Frankfurter sausages
4 crusty bread rolls
8 slices processed cheese
1 (184-g/6½-oz) can pimientos, drained and cut in strips
8 lettuce leaves
150 ml/¼ pint mayonnaise
parsley sprigs

Set the oven at hot (450 F, 230 C, Gas Mark 8) or heat a grill to maximum. Place the Frankfurters in a saucepan and pour over boiling water to cover. Simmer for 5 minutes. Halve the bread rolls. Drain the Frankfurters and cut each in half. Place 2 Frankfurter halves, side by side, on each halved roll and cover with a slice of cheese. Garnish with pimientos and bake in the oven or under the grill, until the cheese has lightly melted. Meanwhile, wash and dry the lettuce leaves and arrange on individual plates. Add a toasted roll and garnish each with a little mayonnaise and a sprig of parsley.

German toasted snack.

German toasted snack

(Illustrated above)

Preparation time: 5-10 minutes

1 level teaspoon cayenne pepper
2 tablespoons whisky
4 slices lean smoked ham, cut to fit toast
1 level teaspoon castor sugar
4 slices bread, lightly toasted
1 (450-g/1-lb) jar sauerkraut
4 slices blue cheese
4 maraschino cherries

Set the oven at hot (230 C, 450 F, Gas Mark 8) or heat a grill to maximum. Stir the cayenne into the whisky and marinate the ham slices in the liquor for a few minutes. Remove and dry on absorbent kitchen paper. Add the sugar to the rest of the marinade and divide among the slices of toast. Place the ham on top and cover each with sauerkraut and cheese. Bake just long enough to allow the cheese to melt. Garnish with a cherry.

Springtime toast

Preparation time: 5-10 minutes

4 large lettuce leaves
4 slices wholewheat, black rye or pumpernickle bread
15 g/½ oz butter
1 teaspoon anchovy paste
2 large tomatoes
150 g/5 oz cottage cheese with chives

Wash the lettuce leaves and pat dry. Lightly toast both sides of the bread. Mix the butter with the anchovy paste and spread on the toast. Wash, dry and slice the tomatoes, removing the cores, and arrange them on top of the toast. Pile each open sandwich with cottage cheese. Serve with a crisp green salad.

Smoked fish toast

Preparation time: 10-15 minutes

4 slices bread
15 g/½ oz butter
2 dessert apples
1 teaspoon lemon juice
½ teaspoon salt
3 teaspoons grated horseradish or horseradish cream
200 g/7 oz smoked trout, mackerel or buckling
50 g/2 oz Cheddar cheese, sliced
2 level teaspoons paprika pepper

Set the oven at hot (230 C, 450 F, Gas Mark 8) or heat a grill to maximum. Toast the bread and spread with the butter. Peel, core and grate the apples, mix with the lemon juice, salt and horseradish and spread the mixture on the buttered toast. Cut the smoked fish into small pieces and divide between the toast. Top with cheese slices. Bake in the oven or under the grill for up to 5 minutes, until the cheese is bubbling. Sprinkle with paprika before serving.

Niçoise toast

(Illustrated opposite)

Preparation time: 10-15 minutes

4 large slices bread
1 clove garlic
15 g/½ oz butter
1 (198-g/7-oz) can tuna
100 g/4 oz cooked French beans
1 (184-g/6½-oz) can pimientos, drained
12 stuffed green olives, halved
8 cocktail onions
1 jar mini sweet corn cobs (optional)
100 g/4 oz Cheddar cheese

Set the oven at hot (230 C, 450 F, Gas Mark 8) or heat a grill to maximum. Lightly toast the bread on both sides. Halve the garlic and use the cut side to rub over the toast, then spread with the butter. Drain the tuna. Divide the beans over the buttered toast and top with the pimientos, halved olives, onions and corn cobs, if used. Flake the tuna with a fork and top each of the open sandwiches. Slice the cheese and place on top. Bake the sandwiches in the oven or under the grill for 5 minutes or until the cheese melts.

Pepper toast

(Illustrated opposite)

Preparation time: 10-15 minutes

4 slices bread
2 small green peppers (see note)
12 stuffed green olives
200 g/7 oz garlic sausage
100 g/4 oz Jarlsberg cheese, grated

Set the oven at hot (230 C, 450 F, Gas Mark 8) or heat a grill to maximum. Lightly toast the bread on both sides. Wash and deseed the peppers, remove the core and cut into rings. Rinse the olives under cold running water, drain well and cut widthways into thin slices. Slice the garlic sausage and arrange on the toast. Cover each slice with pepper rings and grated cheese. Top with sliced olives and place in the oven or under the grill until the cheese melts.

NOTE If cooked or blanched peppers are preferred, bring the rings to the boil in a saucepan of cold water and allow to boil for 1–2 minutes before draining well and arranging over the garlic sausage.

Opposite above: Niçoise toast; *Below:* Pepper toast.

Tuna and shrimp sandwiches

(Illustrated on page 43)

Preparation time: 10-15 minutes

4 large lettuce leaves
4 small sprigs dill or parsley
150 g/5 oz canned tuna
150 g/5 oz canned shrimp, drained
½ onion
1 green pepper
1 teaspoon anchovy paste
15 g/½ oz butter
4 slices wholewheat bread
250 g/9 oz canned artichoke hearts, drained

Rinse the lettuce and dill or parsley under cold running water and drain. Drain the tuna and rinse and drain the shrimp. Peel the onion and cut into rings. Halve the pepper, deseed and cut into rings. Beat the anchovy paste into the butter and spread on the bread slices. Place a lettuce leaf on each buttered slice, top with the tuna and artichoke hearts and then the pepper, onion rings and shrimp. Garnish each sandwich with a sprig of dill or parsley.

Mussel salad on toast

Preparation time: 10-15 minutes

2 eggs, hard-boiled
1 teaspoon lemon juice
2 teaspoons chilli sauce
2 teaspoons gin
1 tablespoon oil
generous pinch each salt, pepper, garlic salt and sugar
100 g/4 oz canned peeled tomatoes
4 large slices bread
2 (100 g/4 oz) cans mussels in brine
2 tablespoons mayonnaise

Shell the eggs, chop the whites and mash the yolks with a fork. Mix the yolks with the lemon juice, chilli sauce, gin, oil, seasonings, sugar and chopped egg white. Drain and chop the tomatoes. Toast the bread on both sides. Drain the mussels and mix with the tomatoes and egg sauce. Spread a little mayonnaise on each slice of toast and top with the salad mixture.

Sausage on toast

(Illustrated opposite)

Preparation time: 10-15 minutes

4 slices bread
6–8 pork or beef sausages
15 g/½ oz butter
½ onion
2 tomatoes
4 slices processed cheese
a little paprika pepper

Set the oven at hot (230 C, 450 F, Gas Mark 8) or heat a grill to maximum. Lightly toast the bread on both sides. Remove the sausage meat from the skins and spread thickly over the toast. Heat the butter in a frying pan and fry the toast with the sausage meat underneath. Remove and keep warm. Peel and cut the onion into rings; slice the tomatoes. In the sausage fat remaining in the pan, quickly fry the onion and tomato and arrange on the toast. Place a slice of cheese on top and bake in the oven or under the grill until the cheese just melts. Garnish with a sprinkling of paprika to serve.

Sausage on toast.

Eggs in piquant sauce

(Illustrated opposite)

Preparation time: 10-15 minutes

8 eggs, hard-boiled
packet instant white sauce to make 1 pint
1–2 teaspoons dry mustard
½ teaspoon castor sugar
1 tablespoon wine vinegar
1 teaspoon grated horseradish or horseradish cream
2 tablespoons chopped parsley

Remove the shell from the eggs and cut each egg in half. Make up the sauce according to the instructions on the packet and stir over the heat while it thickens. Add mustard, to taste, and stir in the sugar, vinegar and horseradish. When the sauce is thoroughly heated, add the halved eggs and carefully heat through without breaking them. Garnish with parsley and serve with mashed potatoes.

Variations

Eggs in savoury tomato sauce Heat 25 g/1 oz butter in a saucepan and add 1 tablespoon flour. Stir with a wooden spoon over a low heat for a few minutes until golden brown. With the pan off the heat, add 1 (150-g/5-oz) can tomato purée and 250 ml/8 fl oz water slowly, stirring continuously. Return to the heat and stir until the sauce has thickened. Season with salt, pepper and paprika. Add 250 ml/8 fl oz tomato juice and 6 tablespoons tomato ketchup, before carefully adding the halved eggs. Heat through before serving. (Illustrated opposite.)

Eggs in curry sauce Melt 25 g/1 oz butter in a saucepan, and stir in 1½ tablespoons flour. Stir with a wooden spoon over a low heat for a few minutes until golden brown. Stir in 2–3 teaspoons curry powder and slowly add 350 ml/12 fl oz stock. Stir continuously over the heat until the sauce thickens. Season with salt and pepper and finally add 250 ml/8 fl oz single cream. Carefully add the halved eggs to heat through before serving. (Illustrated opposite.)

Tomato and bacon omelette

Preparation time: 10-15 minutes

1 (397-g/14-oz) can peeled tomatoes
100 g/4 oz streaky bacon
4 eggs, lightly beaten
25 g/1 oz plain flour
4 tablespoons milk
½ teaspoon salt
¼ teaspoon pepper
1 small onion, chopped and fried until crisp
2 tablespoons chopped parsley

Drain the tomatoes. Chop the bacon and in a covered frying pan, fry over a low heat, in its own fat until crisp. Stir together the eggs, flour, milk and salt to make a runny batter (you may need to add a little water). Pour the batter over the crispy bacon in the pan and allow it to set slightly over the heat for a minute or two. Cover with the drained tomatoes, sprinkle with pepper and the fried onion and garnish with parsley. Replace the lid and cook over low heat for 5 minutes. Serve immediately on a warmed dish accompanied with a crisp green salad.

Clockwise: Eggs in savoury tomato sauce; Eggs in curry sauce; Eggs in piquant sauce (recipes above).

Artichokes with eggs.

Artichokes with eggs

(Illustrated above)

Preparation time: 10-15 minutes

225 g/8 oz canned artichoke bottoms
2 tomatoes
2 tablespoons oil
½ teaspoon salt
¼ teaspoon pepper
4 eggs
2 tablespoons single cream
2 tablespoons tomato purée
2 tablespoons chopped parsley

Drain the artichokes and reserve the liquid. Wash, dry and cut each tomato in half. Heat the oil in a frying pan and fry the artichokes and tomatoes on both sides over a low heat. Mix the salt and pepper and sprinkle half over the tomatoes. Carefully break the eggs into the pan to fry, sprinkling them with the remaining seasoning. Meanwhile, mix the cream with 1 tablespoon of the reserved artichoke liquid, the tomato purée and parsley and pour over the eggs just before serving. Serve with French bread or potato chips.

Continental egg and sausage salad

Preparation time: 15-25 minutes

2 tomatoes
2 eggs, hard-boiled
1 pickled cucumber
1 apple
100 g/4 oz Mortadella or Italian ham sausage
1 tablespoon lemon juice
½ teaspoon salt
generous pinch pepper
50 g/2 oz curd cheese
2 tablespoons single cream
½ teaspoon mild mustard
1 teaspoon grated horseradish or horseradish cream
1 teaspoon sugar
4 large slices bread
2 tablespoons chopped parsley

Make a small incision at the base of each tomato, place in a bowl and pour over boiling water; leave for 1–2 minutes. Shell the eggs and chop. Dice the cucumber; peel, core and dice the apple. Remove the skin from the sausage and dice the meat. Drain the tomatoes, remove the skin, and cut the flesh into small pieces. Mix with the egg, cucumber, apple and sausage. Add the lemon juice and seasoning. Mix together the curd cheese, cream, mustard, horseradish and sugar and fold into the salad ingredients. Lightly toast the bread on both sides and top each slice with the salad, then garnish with parsley. Serve with Haricot bean salad (see page 35) or as a main course with Savoury potato croquettes (see page 32) and a crisp green salad.

NOTE If this dish is prepared a day in advance, keep it covered in a refrigerator and add a little milk before serving.

Spinach pancakes

Preparation time: 15-25 minutes

1 (227-g/8-oz) packet frozen chopped spinach
2 tablespoons double cream
salt and pepper
pinch ground nutmeg
4 eggs
150 ml/¼ pint milk
50 g/2 oz plain flour
2 tablespoons dripping or oil

Heat up the chopped spinach, following the instructions on the packet. Drain thoroughly. Stir in the cream, seasoning and nutmeg and keep warm. Meanwhile, make the pancake batter. Whisk together the eggs and milk and a pinch of salt. Stir in the flour, a little at a time, to prevent lumps. Heat a little of the dripping or oil in a frying pan for each pancake. Pour in a quarter of the batter, and tilt the pan so that the batter covers the base. Allow the batter to set before loosening the sides. Carefully turn the pancake over and cook on the other side until set. Tip the pancake on to a warmed plate and repeat with the remaining fat or oil and batter to make 4 pancakes.

Fill each pancake with the creamed spinach mixture and either roll up or fold over to serve.

Variation

Savoury pancakes may be made with a variety of fillings such as fried chicken livers, canned button mushrooms or fried bacon and served with a crisp green salad. A variety of sweet pancakes can also be made, for dessert. Serve with apple purée and a pinch of ground cinnamon, or spread thickly with jam or simply cover with a mixture of cinnamon and sugar. Fill with slices of baked fruit in season, such as apple, banana, pears or peaches or fill with stewed fruit.

Spanish fried eggs.

Spanish fried eggs

(Illustrated above)

Preparation time: 15-25 minutes

100 g/4 oz streaky bacon
1 onion
1 clove garlic
1 green pepper
4 tomatoes
2 tablespoons chopped parsley
few drops Tabasco sauce
pinch each dried oregano or marjoram and salt
2 (150-g/5-oz) cans prawns, drained
4 eggs

Chop the bacon. Peel and dice the onion; peel and crush the garlic with a little salt. Halve and deseed the pepper, rinse and cut into strips. Wash and dry the tomatoes and cut each into 8. In a frying pan, gently fry the bacon in its own fat, add the onion and garlic and fry together, stirring continuously. Add the pepper, tomato and parsley, cover and simmer for 10 minutes. Mix in the Tabasco, oregano or marjoram and salt and add the prawns. Break the eggs over the vegetable mixture and cook over high heat until the eggs are set. Serve with rye or wholewheat bread.

Cheesy prawn toast

(Illustrated below)

Preparation time: 15-25 minutes

2 (150-g/5-oz) cans prawns
25 g/1 oz butter
4 slices bread
1 (241-g/8½-oz) can asparagus tips
2 egg yolks
100 ml/4 fl oz single cream
40 g/1½ oz cheese, grated
½ teaspoon salt
generous pinch pepper
sprigs of parsley

Set the oven at hot (230 C, 450 F, Gas Mark 8) or heat a grill to maximum. Briefly rinse the prawns under cold running water and drain well. Pat dry on absorbent kitchen paper. Melt half the butter in a frying pan and fry the bread slices on one side only. Remove to an ovenproof dish. In the same frying pan, add the remaining butter and the prawns and heat through for 1 minute, stirring continuously. Drain the asparagus, reserving the liquid. Add the asparagus tips to the prawns and heat through. Mix together the egg yolks, cream, cheese and seasoning, adding a little of the reserved asparagus liquid. Divide the prawn mixture over each untoasted side of the bread and pour over the sauce. Bake in the oven or under the grill for 8–10 minutes, or until the cheese begins to bubble and brown. Garnish with parsley. Serve with a crisp green salad.

Hungarian eggs 'en cocotte'

Preparation time: 15-25 minutes

50 g/2 oz butter
150 g/5 oz smoked ham
1 (100-g/4-oz) piece Edam or Cheddar cheese
4 eggs
salt and pepper
4 tablespoons double cream
4 level teaspoons paprika pepper

Grease 4 cocottes or ramekins with the butter. Dice the ham and the cheese and scatter in the bottom of the dishes. Break an egg into each and season to taste. Beat the cream until just stiff, mix in the paprika and spoon over the eggs. Cover each cocotte with cooking foil, stand in a bain marie or a roasting tin with hot water that just comes half way up the side of the dishes. Place in a moderate oven (160 C, 325 F, Gas Mark 3) for about 15 minutes, or until the eggs are cooked. Serve with toast.

Cheesy prawn toast.

Desserts

Apple snow

Preparation time: 5-10 minutes

3 egg whites
2 level tablespoons powdered glucose
350g/12 fl oz apple purée
juice of ½ lemon
1 tablespoon preserved cranberries

Whisk the egg whites until stiff and fold in the glucose. Mix together the apple purée and lemon juice and fold into the 'snow'. Serve in 4 individual glass bowls topped with a few cranberries.

Cherry nut mousse

Preparation time: 5-10 minutes

3 eggs, separated
1 tablespoon icing sugar
100g/4oz finely-chopped nuts
20 maraschino cherries, rinsed and dried
generous dash cherry brandy or Kirsch

Whisk the egg whites until stiff. Beat the yolks with the icing sugar until frothy and add the nuts. Chop the cherries finely and fold into the yolk mixture with the egg whites. Spoon into 4 individual bowls and chill slightly before serving.

Brandied pears

Preparation time: 5-10 minutes

4 canned pear halves
4 tablespoons preserved cranberries or blackcurrants
1 tablespoon lemon juice
3 tablespoons pear brandy or Kirsch
2 tablespoons desiccated coconut

Arrange the pear halves, cut side down, on 4 plates. Mix together the cranberries or blackcurrants, lemon juice and brandy or Kirsch and pour over the pears. Garnish with coconut before serving.

Orange surprise

Preparation time: 5-10 minutes

2 oranges
1 tablespoon powdered glucose or castor sugar
4 tablespoons advocaat
1 teaspoon coffee essence

Peel the oranges, removing the pith and pips and dice the flesh. Divide among 4 plates and sprinkle each with glucose or sugar. Mix together the advocaat and coffee essence and pour over the oranges to serve.

Apricot cream

(Illustrated on page 16)

Preparation time: 5-10 minutes

500g/1 lb 2 oz canned apricot halves
150 ml/¼ pint white wine
150g/5 oz curd cheese, or cream cheese with a little milk
5 tablespoons double cream
25 g/1 oz desiccated coconut

In a liquidiser, blend together the apricots with their juice and the wine. Blend in the curd or cream cheese and cream. Fill 4 individual bowls and garnish with the coconut.

Variation

Peaches can be used instead of apricots and topped with a few raspberries.

Melon fruit salad.

Melon fruit salad

(Illustrated above)

Preparation time: 5-10 minutes

1 honeydew melon
2 oranges
200 g/7 oz black grapes
juice of 1 lemon
pinch of ground ginger
1 tablespoon sugar, or to taste

Cut the melon in half, lengthways, discard the seeds, scoop out the flesh and cut into cubes. Peel and dice the oranges removing the pips. Wash and drain the grapes, patting them dry with absorbent kitchen paper. Mix together the fruit, adding the lemon juice, ginger and sugar to taste. Pile the fruit back into the hollowed-out melon shells.

Special fruit cocktail

Preparation time: 5-10 minutes

½ teaspoon lemon juice
2 (225-g/8-oz) cans fruit cocktail, drained
4 sponge fingers
75 ml/3 fl oz cherry brandy, fruit brandy (for example, apricot) or orange liqueur
1 tablespoon chopped almonds

Add the lemon juice to the fruit cocktail and spoon into 4 individual glasses or small bowls. Crumble the sponge fingers and sprinkle with the brandy or liqueur. Top each fruit cup with this mixture and sprinkle with chopped almonds.

Variation

Juice from canned or frozen raspberries can be substituted for the brandy.

Vanilla ice cream with hot chocolate sauce

Preparation time: 5-10 minutes

1 (500-ml/17.6-fl oz) carton vanilla ice cream
100 g/4 oz golden syrup
100 g/4 oz plain chocolate

Cut the ice cream into 4 portions and place in individual glasses or bowls. Leave in the refrigerator while making the sauce. Heat together the golden syrup and chocolate in a double boiler until melted and thoroughly blended. To serve, stir the hot chocolate sauce and pour it over the ice cream. Serve immediately.

NOTE A little brandy may be added to the hot chocolate sauce. Also for a ginger sauce, combine 2 tablespoons finely-chopped preserved ginger with about 2 tablespoons of the syrup from the jar. Add to the chocolate sauce.

Ice cream with fruit sauce.

Blackcurrant ice bowl

(Illustrated opposite)

Preparation time: 5-10 minutes

1 (1-litre/35.2-fl oz) carton blackcurrant sorbet
150 ml/$\frac{1}{4}$ pint double cream
100 ml/4 fl oz advocaat
4 ice cream wafers

Cut the sorbet into 4 portions and place in individual glass bowls. Whip the cream until stiff. Pour a little of the advocaat over each ice cream portion and top with a swirl of the whipped cream. Garnish with an ice cream wafer or wafer biscuit and serve immediately.

Ice cream with fruit sauce

(Illustrated left)

Preparation time: 5-10 minutes

25 g/1 oz butter
275 g/10 oz frozen raspberries
50 ml/2 fl oz cherry brandy or Kirsch
1 (1-litre/35.2-fl oz) carton ice cream, flavour according to taste

Melt the butter in a saucepan over low heat, add the raspberries and heat through. Stir in the brandy or Kirsch and heat through. Divide the ice cream between 4 individual glasses or turn out on to a serving dish, and pour hot fruit sauce over before serving.

Blackcurrant ice bowl (recipe above).

Sweet fruit omelette

Preparation time: 15-25 minutes

450 g/1 lb frozen strawberries or raspberries, thawed
50 g/2 oz butter
a little sugar (optional)
6–8 eggs
pinch salt
icing sugar

Put the fruit in a frying pan with 15 g/½ oz of the butter. Add the sugar, if used, cover and warm through over low heat, stirring until the fruit has softened. Meanwhile, in a bowl, whisk together the eggs and salt. Melt the remaining butter in another frying pan. Divide the beaten egg into 4 to make 4 individual omelettes. Allow the underside of each omelette to set before gently loosening the edges. As each one is slipped out on to a plate, fill one half with some of the warmed strawberries and fold the other half over. Dust with icing sugar and serve immediately.

Variation

Instead of strawberries or raspberries, use canned, drained and sliced apricot halves, sliced peaches or canned, drained blackberries or blackcurrants.

Mocha mousse

Preparation time: 15-25 minutes

4 eggs, separated
200 g/7 oz icing sugar
2 level teaspoons instant coffee powder
1 level tablespoon cocoa powder
15 g/1 oz powdered gelatine
2 tablespoons hot water

Whisk the egg whites until stiff. In a double boiler, combine the icing sugar with the egg yolks, coffee and cocoa and stir over a low heat until thick and creamy. Remove from the heat. Dissolve the gelatine in the hot water in a basin over a saucepan of hot water. Blend into the egg yolk mixture and fold in the egg white. Divide the mousse between 4 individual dishes and chill thoroughly before serving.

Cherry meringue pudding

Preparation time: 15-25 minutes

300 ml/½ pint milk
½ vanilla pod
575 g/1 lb 4 oz cooked long-grain rice (see note)
100 g/4 oz castor sugar
500 g/1 lb 2 oz canned morello cherries, drained and stoned
25 g/1 oz butter
4 egg whites
slivered almonds (optional)

Set the oven at hot (230 C, 450 F, Gas Mark 8) or heat a grill to maximum. In a saucepan, gently heat the milk with the vanilla pod. Once the milk starts to simmer, remove the vanilla pod, add the cooked rice and stir over a low heat until the milk has been absorbed. Add 25 g/1 oz of the sugar and most of the cherries, reserving a few for decoration. Grease a 600 ml/1 pint pudding basin with a little of the butter and fill with the rice mixture. Chill thoroughly in the refrigerator for 2 hours to set. Grease a shallow ovenproof dish with the remaining butter and turn out the rice pudding. Whisk the egg whites until stiff and fold in the remaining sugar. Cover the rice mould with the meringue and decorate with slivered almonds, if used. Place in the oven or under the grill for 2–3 minutes until the meringue begins to brown. Serve decorated with the reserved cherries.

NOTE For 575 g/1 lb 4 oz cooked rice, use 175 g/6 oz uncooked rice.

Yogurt

Yogurt is a very useful and versatile ingredient because it is rich in protein but relatively low in calories. The following recipes can be prepared in 5–10 minutes.

Pineapple yogurt

Preparation time: 5-10 minutes

1 (225-g/8-oz) can crushed pineapple
1 tablespoon lemon juice
1 tablespoon honey
2 (142-ml/5-fl oz) cartons natural yogurt
4 sponge fingers

In an electric mixer, combine the pineapple with the juice from the can, the lemon juice, honey and yogurt. Crumble the sponge fingers into the bottom of 4 individual bowls before adding the yogurt.

Apple yogurt

Preparation time: 5-10 minutes

250 ml/8 fl oz apple purée
2 (142-ml/5-fl oz) cartons natural yogurt
2 tablespoons blackcurrant syrup or concentrated blackcurrant drink
2 egg whites
1 tablespoon icing sugar
few small dry almond macaroons (optional)

Using an electric mixer, combine the apple purée, yogurt and syrup. In a separate bowl, whisk the egg whites until stiff, and stir in the icing sugar. Fold the sweetened egg whites into the yogurt mixture and serve in 4 individual bowls. Garnish with macaroons, if used.

Variation

As an alternative to apple purée, use 2 peeled, cored and grated apples and continue as above.

Hazelnut yogurt

Preparation time: 5-10 minutes

2 (142-ml/5-fl oz) cartons natural yogurt
200 g/7 oz hazelnuts, chopped
2 egg yolks
2 tablespoons powdered glucose or castor sugar

Mix 1 carton yogurt with the remaining ingredients. When thoroughly combined, add the rest of the yogurt and mix well. Serve in 4 individual bowls.

Curd cheese

Curd cheese is a versatile medium-fat cheese that is readily available and becoming very popular. Cream cheese can be substituted in the following recipes; however, remember cream cheese has more calories. All these desserts are prepared in 5–10 minutes.

Curd cheese with peaches

Preparation time: 5-10 minutes

2 whole fresh, or 3 canned peach halves
1 teaspoon lemon juice
200 g/7 oz curd cheese
1 tablespoon honey
2 tablespoons single cream

If using fresh peaches, peel and chop into small chunks. If using canned peach halves, drain and chop. Sprinkle with lemon juice to prevent discoloration. Combine all the ingredients and serve in 4 individual bowls.

Variations

Instead of peaches, use apricots (fresh, canned or dried and soaked) or stoned and halved plums.

Banana curd cheese

Preparation time: 5-10 minutes

200 g/7 oz curd cheese
½–1 tablespoon powdered glucose, or to taste
1 tablespoon milk
1 teaspoon honey
2 egg whites
1 banana
1 teaspoon lemon juice

Mix together the curd cheese, glucose, milk and honey in a bowl. Whisk the egg whites until stiff and fold carefully into the cheese mixture. Peel and slice the banana and sprinkle with lemon juice to prevent discoloration. Fold into the curd mixture and serve in 4 individual glasses or bowls.

Variation

Add a little cooked rhubarb to the banana for extra flavour; or a few chopped toasted nuts for a contrast in texture. If using a very ripe banana, mash with a fork before sprinkling with lemon juice.

Orange curd cheese

Preparation time: 5-10 minutes

1 large orange
200 g/7 oz curd cheese
1 teaspoon lemon juice
1 tablespoon castor sugar
2 tablespoons single cream

Peel the orange, remove any pith and cut into segments. Combine with all the remaining ingredients and serve in 4 individual bowls.

Wine and lemon cream

Preparation time: 5-10 minutes

150 ml/¼ pint white wine
150 ml/¼ pint water
1 (69-g/2.4-oz) packet vanilla instant dessert whip
1 (142-ml/5-fl oz) carton natural or lemon yogurt
rind of 1 lemon and juice of ½ lemon
few drops yellow food colouring (optional)
150 ml/¼ pint double cream, whipped
1 tablespoon chopped pistachio nuts
thin lemon slices to garnish

In a bowl, mix together the wine and water. Add the dessert whip and whisk vigorously for about 1 minute, until the mixture thickens. Stir in the yogurt, lemon rind and juice and the food colouring, if used. Pour into 4 individual glass bowls and chill slightly. Decorate with swirls of the whipped cream, a sprinkling of nuts and a few lemon slices.